The Friendship of Women

A Spiritual Tradition

JOAN CHITTISTER

Icons by Marcie Bircher

SHEED & WARD

Franklin, Wisconsin

and

 *Benetvision*

Erie, Pennsylvania

Icons © 2000 Marcie Bircher
Text © 2000 Joan D. Chittister

SHEED & WARD

7373 South Lovers Lane Road
Franklin, Wisconsin 53132
1-800-266-5564
www.sheedandward.com

ISBN 1-58051-101-5

An apostolate of the Priests of the Sacred Heart, a Catholic religious
congregation, the mission of Sheed & Ward is to publish books of
contemporary impact and enduring merit in Catholic Christian thought
and action. The books published, however, reflect the opinion of their
authors and are not meant to represent the official position of the
Priests of the Sacred Heart.

Benetvision

355 East Ninth St.
Erie, PA 16503-1107
814-459-5994
www.eriebenedictines.org
e-mail: msbpr@juno.com

ISBN: 1-890890-10-3

01 02 03 04 05   5 4 3 2

Table of Contents

It takes a lot of friends
to write a book about friendship.
I'm grateful to all of them.

———————————————

Introduction

FRIENDSHIP COLORS the very air we breathe. It is everywhere around us. We can see it in the eyes of old women in the kitchens of the women they love. We can hear it in the voices of one young woman giggling to another over a telephone. We can feel it beating in our own hearts on lonely rainy days in far away places when, most alone, we are haunted by the memory of those who have walked through life with us and walk with us still. Friendship binds past and present and makes bearable the uncertainty of the future.

But friendship is, at best, an elusive concept, a movable feast. The word itself shifts in meaning from historical period to historical period. The definition of it shifts from person to person, from relationship to relationship. The category splits and shades and nuances almost into oblivion at times. Friendship, we know, is sometimes "best" and sometimes "good." It is often "casual" and commonly "occasional." It ranges from the mellow to the saturating. It is no single thing ever and yet there is no doubt of what it is when we have it.

The question of the place and nature and value of friendship has been, over the centuries, the fascination of philosophers, the quandary of psychologists, the invisible sacrament of which theologians spoke and the grail of mystics and poets. Whatever the context out of which the discussion springs, friendship is, in the end, always and everywhere eternal mystery, eternal desire. It is a grasp at the ultimate, the quest for human understanding.

"TWO ARE BETTER than one," the Book of Ecclesiastes teaches, "for if they fall, the one will lift the other up; but woe to the one that is alone...."[1] It's a simple statement, a profound one, this biblical commonplace. But the conventional wisdom of a highly mobile, basically anonymous, totally fragmented society affects, at least, to ignore it. "No one is indispensable," we say so flippantly, so unfeelingly in a massified culture. But the words grate like sandpaper on the soul of the wizened and the loving. The sophisticates who say them are able, in this whirl of isolates, to pawn themselves off as wise and humble, even holy, for the claiming of them. The fact is, though, that the saying is woefully, pitiably, glaringly wrong. In the face of Ecclesiastes it simply shrivels away in the hold of a more searing and truer truth.

There is indeed one thing that renders all of us, any of us, indispensable. As long as there is someone, somewhere whose life breathes in time with my own, I know down deep that I am indeed needed, that I have no right to die. I know that I am truly indispensable, irreplaceable, vital to a life beyond my own. To that person I am indispensable. Whatever my own needs, the love of the other has greater claim on me than I do on myself. Our friends depend on us. Cicero wrote of his own sorrow at the death of his friend, Scipio: "I have been bereaved of a friend," he says, "such as the world will never see again….(But) I do not feel that Scipio has suffered any misfortune; I am the one who has suffered misfortune."[2]

TO HAVE A FRIEND is to acknowledge that some part of someone else's life which we have held tenderly, trustingly in our own hands might well die with us. Where does grief for the dead come from, in fact, if not from the anger and sense of abandonment that emerges from the realization that some part of ourselves has been taken away from us without our permission? Grief is simply a measure of the joy, the depth that comes from growing to know another and letting them know me in ways in which I am exposed to no one else.

Indeed, to lose a friend is to be cast back into the insularism that is the self. It is a dark and sniveling place to be. It is a dangerous place to be, narrow and confined by the limits of the self. Only friendship can really save us from our own smallness.

But first, of course, there are things to consider: What exactly is a friend? Is friendship really possible? Is friendship a necessary good or simply a social filler? Is friendship spiritual? Isn't God alone enough? What, if anything, does friendship have to do with living life forever on the brink of becoming?

THERE IS A LONG answer and a short one to the question of what friendship has to do with personal development and spiritual growth. The short answer is "Everything"— if, that is, we are to believe the thinkings of the philosophers, the findings of modern psychology, as well as the witness of history and the wisdom of Ecclesiastes. The long answer comes in the slowly dawning awareness that once we are loved we have an obligation to live as best we can. Once we have discovered the love that doubles life but does not consume it, we must live so that the other, who

walks by the light within us as well as the light within herself, may not proceed befuddled by our own failure to illuminate the way. The love of a friend comes always with a lantern in its hand.

By love I am not talking about passion, though that will certainly, in one energizing sense or another, be a fortifying dimension of any deep and good relationship. By love I am talking about the process of melting into the life of another in ways that fuse our souls, open our hearts and stretch our minds, and all the while claiming nothing in return. Friendship is the process of opening ourselves to the care, to the wisdom, of the other. The love of friendship is the love that holds no secrets, has no unasked questions, no unspoken thoughts, no unanswered concerns. Friendship extends us into places we have not gone before and cannot go alone.

Friendship may be either ultimate or commonplace, but it is never without the gain of a little more self.

THE HISTORY of friendship has been an obscure one in every dimension, but most of all, for women. In the manner of just about everything else in life, friendship has been a male preserve. Montaigne, as late as the 16th century, wrote in his essay "On Friendship" that "…the normal capacity of women is, in fact, unequal to the demands of that communion and intercourse on which the sacred bond (of friendship) is fed; their souls do not seem firm enough to bear the strain of so hard and lasting a tie."[3] Montaigne was not original, not isolated, in his thinking. He had centuries of philosophy on which to base his statement.

The ancients—Plato and Aristotle and the schools of philosophy to follow them—assumed that friendship was one of the higher acts of the human soul and that males, the highest creature in the hierarchy of creation, would choose their equals, other males, to be their friends. Friends were the glue of the nation, the network of political allies, associations, loyalties, and collaborations on which rested the decisions of the state.[4]

Cicero, the great Roman orator, wrote his classic essay "On Friendship" not as a tribute to personal affection but as a final attempt to save the failing Republic of Rome from encroaching monarchy and dictatorship by reviving the democratic networks that rested on shared ideals, on personal relationships.[5]

In later Middle Ages the word "friend" included relatives as well as any associates or benefactors or public patrons who could be counted on for the alliances it might take to secure the power and property of the family.[6] Friends were, for the most part in this society, simply "connections."[7] Since such political concerns were not the realm of women and since most women were confined to the arena of the family, neither was friendship a woman's domain. In fact, only in our own century has the privatization of friendship become common social currency.

AND YET, IT IS EQUALLY true that there is throughout history another deeper, more personal tradition of spiritual friendship than the alliances of the court and the castle. There is another current, plain for us to see, running parallel to this political dimension. There is another model of friendship besides the conventional model of male friendship from which we can draw to measure the quality of our own, if we only have the eyes to see it.

Philosophers and leaders in the spiritual life wrestled with the idea of friendship from century to century. Aristotle himself said, "What is a friend? A single soul dwelling in two bodies."[8] And Catullus, in one of the most moving eulogies to a friend ever given says of the relationship, "Our soul is buried, mine with yours entwined."[9] No mere political connections here.

The desert monastics understood the role of spiritual friendship and considered it an essential part of the spiritual life even when they exalted *apathaeia*—passionlessness—and warned against the distractions of human attachments. The mandate of hospitality brought these spiritual guardians to attend to the physical as well as the spiritual needs of those whom they saw as their spiritual disciples.[10]

Saint Ambrose saw human friendship as a necessary part of the outpouring of God's friendship. "Because God is true," Ambrose argues, "friends can be true.... Because God offers friendship, we can be each other's friends."[11]

Saint Augustine assumed community and human relationships as the ground of growth. "The more friends I shall have," he wrote, "the more can we love wisdom in common."[12]

Saint Benedict considered the manifestation of the self to another as a fundamental step on the path to full human development. [13]

THE TRADITION WAS an unfailing one: friendship became the mucilage of the Christian community and reached its highpoint in the spiritual writings of the Cistercian monk and abbot, Aelred of Riveaulx, who dedicated his life to the subject. In the twelfth century he wrote a theology of friendship that derived from the thesis that "God is friendship." To Aelred, friendship was a necessary dimension of the Christian life and a particular dimension of an individual's spiritual awareness, as well.[14]

These views of the spiritual life did not, in the long run, prevail. In the face of a stream of social catastrophes, the God of Love became God the Judge and Jesus the Lord. Negative asceticism, repentance, constraint—all designed to atone for the kind of sin that could generate such godly wrath— became the temper of the time.[15] During the same period, the influence of women on idea development and their public visibility diminished even more with the rise of the all-male university system. Cut off from the developing academic world, whatever experience, whatever insights, women might have brought to the subject were lost behind the cloister walls of convents and castles and kitchens. Friendship went its merry, male way, the stuff of male poets and essayists, perhaps, but not the coin of the realm and definitely not a woman's prerogative.

UNTIL NOW. Until our time. Until, that is, the release of energy that came with women's new awareness of themselves led women to speak of their own experiences. Until psychology began the analysis of human relationships and discovered, lo and behold, that relationship was of the essence of being woman. Until we discovered the place of talk in the development of human community and a woman's healing gift for it. Then we began to look back on history with new eyes. Then we began to see, as if for the first time, the women who had mothered our hopes and had proclaimed their presence as women and had demonstrated their connection to each other and to God. Then we began to see one another with new eyes. Then we discovered what it was to be a woman with other women. "Each friend," Anais Nin writes, "represents a world in us, a world possibly not born until they arrive, and it is only by this meeting that a new world is born."[16]

Friendship in general, women's friendships in particular, has become a topic of value again. Friendship is coming to life in a new way in our own time. And it is coming to life most clearly in women. The question is what qualities sustain it and where shall we look to find them if we are to live all the worlds for which we have been made. Women themselves tell us now what they look for in friendship and scripture shows us instances where these very qualities in women have changed the world. It is time to honor both of them.

"My friends," writes the poet Emily Dickinson, "are my estate."[17] Friends are, in other words, the only thing I will have at the end. My friends will be the treasure I accrue in life and a measure, perhaps, of my own worth, as well. It is surely, then, of the highest spiritual order to celebrate the Sacrament of Friendship.

The Lydia Factor:

Models for Growth

"NO SOUL IS DESOLATE," George Eliot wrote, "as long as there is a human being for whom it can feel trust and reverence."[18] The comment deserves serious consideration. It brings us to rethink the whole notion of friendship. If Eliot is correct, then a friendship is more than an element of social life. It is a spiritual force that touches the soul.

The fact is that companionship is not enough to fill a life. What is needed in human relationships above all, if they are to give substance to our lives, is the quality of fusion, the character of meld. It is the challenge of connection. It is an insight of grave consequence in a world where we can live in crowds forever and never even notice that we are alone. It is so easy to think that we have friends and know how to be a friend when all we really have are contacts. It is so easy to think we have a relationship with someone when all we really have is more or less time for idle conversations with people we see often but keep at a distance always.

Where there is no reverence, no trust, there may be attraction but there is no friendship. It is a social question of major import in the great anonymous society in which we live, where neighbors do not know neighbors and telephones have answering machines to weed out calls.

THE UNDERLYING TENSION in contemporary Western society is the struggle between the public and the personal. We are a private people who happen to live in groups. We are individuals who develop communities based more on the rights of each separate member than on our obligations to the groups themselves. We prize autonomy as we honor little else. And yet, nothing has become more apparent in the advance toward personal independence than the inextricable connection between human relationship and mental health. Women who have friends, who trust and reverence someone, are, we know now, simply healthier, happier people.[19] They're more responsive to others, more secure about themselves. Friends open new worlds for us and invite us in, laughing and singing. Friends carry our burdens in their own hearts and give us the wisdom of distance to deal with them. Friends, the people we really trust, point a way.

The question is how to balance independence and relationship. What is it we need in order to come out of ourselves without at the same time losing ourselves in the interests and ideas, the plans and pursuits of the other? It's a difficult question in a society of gurus who offer new feel-good fixes by the day. But whatever the latest fashion in self-development, there is always, for the woman who looks for root in the tried and true, the memory of Lydia. To understand friendship and its place in the life of a woman, we need to maintain the memory of Lydia.

LYDIA, WHOM SCRIPTURE credits, along with Paul, for the implantation of Christianity in Europe, is clearly a strong and independent woman, unusual for her time.[20] Unusual perhaps for any time. The data we have about the woman Lydia may be sparse but it is clear. She was a woman of substance. She was strong-minded and she was self-directing.

There is no mention of a husband in the scripture that describes Lydia, no mention of family chores, no hint of dependence. No sheltered small town girl, this one. On the contrary. Lydia came from a bustling commercial area once itself called "Lydia." It was an urban gateway between East and West, a crossroads of ideas, cultures and business. Lydia had experience. She had traveled. She knew more about life than the boundaries of the clan and the certainties of the countryside. Lydia had seen things of which most women of her time had never even dreamed. And she gathered these women around her and opened to them a whole new way of thinking about the world.

LYDIA WAS, THE SCRIPTURE says, "a seller of purple." She did business, in other words, with the kind of people who made clothes for kings or dyes for local industries. She was not a street vendor. She was not a hired hand. This woman had influence and she used it. She "constrained" Paul, the epistle points out, to stay in her house, to make his first congregation in Europe a congregation of women. Lydia was not the average woman.[21]

She was, in fact, just the kind of woman anyone would want for a friend. She was someone to be looked up to, someone whose timbre could be reckoned. Lydia did what she set out to do. Lydia could be trusted.

In the Lydias of the world lies the self-confidence that magnetizes others, that draws people to them, that gives a sense of security and a touch of excitement to the lives of those around them. She was a seeker who swept others along in the passion of her pursuits and made the going worthwhile if for no other reason than the exhilaration of the search. She was a free woman who freed other women around her. In Lydia, a woman could see what she herself wanted to become. She could develop a sense of belonging. She

The role of Lydia is to lead us beyond herself.

could explore new notions in safe space and without disdain.

THE LYDIA FACTOR of friendship is the desire to draw from another the strength we need to go beyond where we would ever go alone. We search for a Lydia in our lives to give us the courage to walk on tightropes above raging cataracts of confusion below us. With Lydias to lead the way, we can do anything. We can open ourselves to new ideas and risk the beckoning unknown.

There is a problem with looking for Lydia, however. The role of Lydia is to lead us beyond herself. When we find ourselves walking only in the shadow of the Lydias in our lives rather than beside them we have substituted dependence for friendship. It is so easy to mistake one for the other but the signs are clear. The real Lydias, when we finally find them, are not those who remake us in their image. They are those who enable us to become the best of what we can be, to develop who we are in ourselves, who see our ideas as just as valuable, just as possible, as their own. The Lydias around us don't enslave us to their ideas. They provide the environment, the model, that leads us to think on our own. In that kind of strength lies the glory of friendship.

The Lydias around us . . .
provide the environment,
the model,
that leads us
to think on our own.

The Prisca Factor:

Confirmation of the Self

"**NEVER CONTRACT** friendship," Confucius said, "with anyone who is not better than yourself."[22] The idea may be sound but, given its ancient origin, the idea must be at least suspect, if not spurious. The problem is that friendship as social convention has changed from one age to the other. In ancient Greece, the friend was a political ally.[23] In medieval France to talk about friendship was, in large part, really to be making a comment on the solidarity of the extended family. In feudal times it meant patronage. In some ages and cultures it has meant comradeship or some kind of institutionalized formal relations between families.[24] Clearly, what each of these ages might have meant by choosing for a friend someone who is superior could indeed have various motives and various meanings. But not now.

In modern times, thanks to the focus on the individual and personal development, the idea of friendship has become part of the subject of the self. Friendship—what we mean by it, how we deal with it—at this time in this society has something to do with what it means to be me. My friends become an extension of myself. They reflect what I think about, what I want in life, what has meaning to me, what kind of depth I have. The truth is that the friends we make have something to do with the women we are, the human beings we are becoming.

Whatever Confucius' motives may have been in advising people of his time to look for friends in which they recognized qualities superior to their own, the advice has its own kind of value now. In an age in which we live like strangers in a strange world, far from family ties, borne along from one shifting institution to another, friendship ceases to be simply a series of social contacts and becomes some kind of lifeline. Friends become our substitutes for the families, the institutions, the ideas we have been forced, for whatever reasons, to leave behind. Then the words of Confucius take on added meaning. Then we realize that we have to determine what it is to be superior and what it means for the shaping of our own lives. Then the memory of Prisca becomes spiritual injunction.

PRISCA WAS A WOMAN who knew hardship and survived it. When the emperor Claudius drove the Jews out of Rome, she had been forced to leave ev-eryone she knew, to relinquish everything she held dear, to forego all the security, all the warmth that the familiar gives. She was a refugee in a stable society, forced to begin again, required against her will to start life over in new territory with new people. She had been uprooted, displaced, left to fend for herself in a society where kinship was key to security. And she survives it all. She even reaches out to take other outcasts in.

Prisca and her husband, Aquila, two tentmakers, meet another tentmaker, Paul of Tarsus, who is making a second missionary journey to areas outside of Judea. They open their home to him, scripture says, and for two years,

The Lydias of our lives stretch the self; the Priscas of our lives confirm the self.

travel with him as missionaries themselves. They begin the first house church in the city of Corinth and, sure of the truth they feel in their hearts, contest with Apollos, a speaker of no small skill but limited background who has been teaching in the local synagogue and they "instruct him more accurately."[25] She is teacher, leader, missionary, all of which have emerged where they would be least likely to be found: in a refugee, a tentmaker and a woman.

AND WHAT DOES that have to do with my choice of friends? More, perhaps, than I have ever realized. Prisca is mentioned six times in scripture, four of them prior to the naming of her husband, the kind of recognition that is unheard of for a woman of the time. Prisca is, in other words, a person in her own right. Prisca is not defined by anything around her or outside of her. Whatever her own lack of supports, of firm ground on which to take her place in the security of the system around her, she speaks her own truth in her own name and she is respected for it.

Prisca is the sign of all the untapped resources within the coarsest craters of the human heart. In her I recognize the one who has the capacity to draw from the well of the self when there is every reason in the world to believe that the well must certainly be dry.

THE PRISCA FACTOR of friendship is the dream of finding in myself the same kind of hidden qualities that I have recognized in another. It is a choice to mine myself to the depth, beyond the limits of what I am inclined to think are the boundaries of my existence. The woman Prisca—exiled, unlettered, simple—reminds me to value the friend who has talents I seek but have yet to develop. She is the prism through which I can catch sight of my own better self.

There is a thin line, however, between admiring what we know to be superior to ourselves and giving way to the despair that the superiority of another can engender. It takes great strength to be a self in the shadow of those whose self seems, at first sight, to be so much greater than my own. But unless I aspire to become the quality of the best people around me, I am doomed either to stay what I am or to seek out the companionship of those who can only ignore my limitations or, worse, validate them. "Tell me what company you keep," Cervantes says, "and I'll tell you what you are."[26] To be our best selves we must keep company with those whom we ourselves know to be better than we are.

FRIENDSHIP IS THE sacrament of possibility. It is trusting that those for whom I care and who say they care for me will reveal to me what I cannot see in myself and prod it to its fullness. The Lydias of our lives stretch the self; the Priscas of our lives confirm the self.

The search for the superior in others is the search for the superior in myself. It is the magnet in the heart that leads us to aspire to levels higher than the watermarks of the culture in which I have been bred. My friend is the one who shows me what I, too, can become if I only set myself to be it.

---

*Prisca . . .
is the prism
through which I can catch sight
of my own better self.*

The Phoebe Factor:

Support in Hard Times

"FRIENDSHIP," KAHLIL Gibran wrote, "is always a sweet responsibility, never an opportunity."[27] To the person who goes through life making the "connections" that promise the right committee appointments, guarantee the plum promotions or assure the regular invitations to all the best cocktail parties of life, Gibran's observation is a confusing one. After all, isn't the purpose of making the right friends to get to the right places and meet the right people? The two positions—Gibran's spiritual dictum and society's pragmatic one—reflect two very distinct worldviews, both of them real, both of them true to a certain degree. But the snag in the game of friendship is that the word "friend" itself is often used so loosely.

Unfortunately, friendship comes in varieties that merge and blur, confuse and contradict one another. A friend is, to many, any of a battery of things: an acquaintance, an associate, a comrade, a compatriot, a childhood companion, an adult peer, a long-standing fellow traveler in a common enterprise. Obviously, the real character of any friendship depends on the mind of the person who is defining it. Contemporary research has divided and subdivided friendships into at least five different levels: from "best" friend to "casual acquaintance," from "friendships of commitment" to "friendships of convenience."[28] Clearly, to say "We've been friends for years" is to say everything and to say nothing at the same time.

SO HOW DO WE tell one kind of friendship from the other? And, in the end, does it make any difference? Really? After all, friendships among women have never been much defined under any circumstances. The classic literature of great eras all record myths of heroic male friendships: Achilles and Patroclus, each of whom fought in behalf of the other; Damon and Pythias, who begged to die for one another; David and Jonathan, who loved each other despite the fact that Saul, Jonathan's father, sought to kill David; Aelred and Richard, twelfth century Cistercian monks who reshaped the thinking of medieval monasticism on the spiritual dimensions of friendship. The relationship of man-to-man was a given but not even the fairy tales recalled great friendships among women. The point was clear: Women did not need women friends. Women needed men.

Not until the mid-1970s did modern psychology even bother to ask in any scientific way whether or not women had friendships at all. As late as 1969, in fact, the social scientist Tiger argued that women were not genetically programmed to bond with one another.[29] But then the floodgates opened. For the next twenty years, human development departments everywhere concentrated on the character and role of friendships among women. The findings completely reversed the philosophical assumptions of centuries. Researchers found a linkage between women's better health, longer life span, resistance to stress, and successful life transitions to the presence of close, confidante relationships in their lives.[30] By 1984, social scientists were suggesting that friendships between women actually maintain marital structures by enabling the women to create personal space and autonomy within the family arena, and historians were now studying the woman-to-woman bond that had created convents, mobilized women's social resistance groups, sustained women in harems and built Be-guinages in Europe.[31] But how can any of it be explained? The answer is getting clearer every day: What bonds women is the enduring echo of Phoebe in every woman's soul. In Phoebe is the seed of great friendship, deep feeling.

PHOEBE GETS ONLY two lines in all of scripture and they are, at first glance, apparently innocuous ones. Paul says of her by way of introducing her to the fledgling little church in Rome to whom she has traveled hundreds of miles to deliver his epistle for him: *I commend to you our sister Phoebe, a deacon of the church at Cenchreae, so that you may welcome her in the Lord as is fitting for the saints, and help her in whatever she may require from you, for she has been a benefactor of many and of myself as well.*[32]

Phoebe was a "deacon"—one who serves, a "sister"—one who loves, and "a benefactor"—one who lives to support the dreams of others which she makes her own. Phoebe was, in other words, a loving presence, a selfless doer, an altruist of souls. She poured her life out on others like oil from an alabaster jar. She healed and served and cared and carried all the burdens of all the people around her. Phoebe freed people to be who they were by attending to what they themselves needed. And she did it at great cost to herself. She "put herself out" as my grandmother used to say. She gave herself away.

THE PHOEBE FACTOR in friendship is the quiet constancy that gives life its composition. The Phoebes of life hold the world together. These are the friends who never miss sending the birthday cards, who call just to "see how you are," who bring the casserole when you're tired, who take the children for a ride to give you some time to yourself, who listen while you talk, who help you hold up your end of the sky.

The Phoebe factor in friendship requires us to be self-contained: she became an independent woman, but not self-centered. She does not become herself for her own sake only. Phoebe reminds us that we do not exist for ourselves alone but she does not call us to efface ourselves. She simply compels us to be about more than ourselves. Friendship, we see in Phoebe, obligates us to the good of the other but does not deny us the obligation at the same time to be the fullness of the self.

The Phoebes in our lives call us to be conscious of the needs around us. When asked, women say repeatedly that a friend "is someone I can call on for help."[33] The Phoebe element in friendship makes the world a better place, a compassionate place, a place where friendship flourishes.

PHOEBE IS A warning as well as a witness. She calls us to realize that to be a Phoebe is not to be a sycophant. Phoebe does not live to defer. She was a "deacon," an identified minister of the church. She is not a member of some eternal servant class. She is not the "female female" whose lot in life is to be the caretaker of the human race because she is not capable of doing anything else. Phoebe is the friend who by being what we need when we need her, reminds us that our own gifts of self are meant to be developed for the sake of the universe. The Phoebe factor in friendship reminds us that we are not servants; we, too, are raised up to be co-creators of the cosmos we call life. For as Alexander Pope said, "I think the way to have a public spirit is first to have a private one: For who the devil can believe that anyone can care for a hundred thousand people who never cared for one?"[34]

The Phoebes of life
hold the world together.

28

The Martha of Bethany Factor:

Experience

"**WHEN A WOMAN** tells the truth," Adrienne Rich writes, "she creates the possibility for more truth around her."[35] And Plutarch, centuries before, agreed. "I want a friend," he said, "who will follow me only in obedience to truth."[36] It is a hard saying. It takes all the marshmallow, all the frills out of human relationships. It brings human communion to the bar of nobility. It is the first principle of real friendship.

Those who prattle conventional wisdom but never speak their own are dangerous people to have around. To call one of them "friend" is worse. If we really believed that such parroting were of the essence of friendship, we could be inclined to trust them. But women don't. One of the most clearly defined dimensions of friendship by women is a "sense of reliable alliance" and the opportunity to "obtain guidance."[37] Women want more in a friend, in other words, than someone with whom they can simply idle away some time. They want someone on whom they can count and someone who will tell them the truth.

TRUTH IS A STRANGE thing, however. It has as many definitions, as many shades, as friendship itself. There is truth that can be counted, for instance. The fact that a thousand people like eggs and one does not may well be a mathematical truth but one that is at best incomplete. What is the real truth of the statement: that eggs are universally good or that it must be said that they are not equally satisfactory to everyone? The question is a crucial one if truth is really to be honored and friendship is really to be true.

There is a difference between fact and truth. The problem is that for far too long, perhaps, much of what is only fact has been allowed to pass for the fullness of truth. It is facile to allow a facet of the truth to speak for all the truth about a subject. Truth has many faces. There is truth that can be tested and found to be either true or false. There is the truth of history and the truth of tradition and the truth of authority and the truth of social expectations. Indeed, there are facts aplenty to press down upon a woman's head. But there is very little of a woman's truth that has been dignified by its inclusion in the pantheon of ethical realities. Instead, women have been told for centuries what someone else said was sin for them and good for them and necessary for them and essential to them and then told that it was all truth. It was true, women were told, that to refuse conjugal relations was sin for them, that self-sacrifice was good for them, that obedience to men was necessary for them, and that the modesty defined by men was essential to their integrity. The fact is that some people sincerely thought so. The truth is, also, however, that some people knew otherwise but were never asked. Indeed, unless the facts pressed down upon a woman's head are also a woman's truth, too, it is at best a truth that is pitifully partial.

BUT ANOTHER TRUTH keeps roiling around in the human psyche, disappearing only to reemerge from century to century in women. There is more truth than they have been traditionally told. Now women want to know a woman's truth. They want to hear from women who do not like eggs. They have come to realize that just because we have a fact that is true does not mean that it is universal truth.

Women are beginning to value the truth, the experience, of other women. They are beginning to recognize the cry of Martha of Bethany. Martha of Bethany knew both fact and truth. She knew for a fact that women were not allowed to study the Torah and she let both her sister and Jesus understand, as she watched him instructing her in it, whatever the warnings of the Law, that she was seeing the tradition of exclusion crumbled by them. She also knew the truth. On the road to Bethany, just as surely as Peter makes a confession of faith in Jesus as messiah, it is also Martha who says to Jesus, "I know that you are the messiah."[38] Her experience has told her what the rabbis would not admit. Her insights have penetrated what the eyes of the system did not see. Her heart has heard what the ears of the pharisees could not hear. Martha of Bethany is a truth-teller.

THE MARTHA FACTOR in friendship makes it plain that women have a truth to tell that is their own. It gives a woman the confidence it takes to claim her own experience and it leads her to seek out, to trust, the truths inside the women around her. Martha of Bethany calls women to see themselves as architects of the faith as well as its consumers.

It is truth in a friendship that gives it depth, and truth that makes it whole. It is truth that drives us to explore ourselves as well as the other, the other as well as ourselves. Truth makes possible the exposure of the soul and the riches of experience. It validates a person's life. What I have come to know may not be universal knowledge, if there is any such thing, but it is my knowledge and that is more than enough to kindle my growing and the growth of others, as well.

THE DARK SIDE of truth is brutality, a word unkindly, untimely said. It is often inflicted in the name of friendship but must never be confused with it. Brutality is never truth. It is, at best, the petty side of a fact. Most of all, brutality is never the stuff of friendship. Oliver Wendell Holmes wrote: "Leave your friend to learn unpleasant things from enemies; they are ready enough to tell them."[39] There are those who would argue that it is precisely the function of friendship to be the bearer of the hostile and the scathing. But there is already too much of that in life to claim for it a role in the rank of friendship. The function of the one who loves me is to enable me to bear the hard truth, to cope with it, to learn from it and to survive it. Not to be the first to say it. "A friend," a Near East proverb teaches, "is one who warns you."[40]

The Martha factor of friendship brings a woman's experience out of the dark night of oblivion into the light of new understandings. It brings women to the point of dignity and gives dignity to women. Any woman who honors the truth within her frees the woman she calls friend to discover for herself what is behind the next question, the next absolute, the next order, the next sin that is committed in the name of God. Any friendship that traffics in the truths of life is surely a holy one.

Martha of Bethany
calls women
to see themselves
as architects of the faith
as well as
its consumers.

The Veronica Factor:

Presence

"WHAT IS THE OPPOSITE of two?" Richard Wilbur wrote, "A lonely me; a lonely you."[41] There may be no more poignant line in literature. The very thought of finding ourselves alone, cut off from the touch of a warm hand, left without a strong shoulder, bereft of the presence of the one who matters, terrifies us to the core. Who of us really wants to go into the darkness of pain or hurt or fear alone? Who of us really wants to go into the light of joy and celebration alone?

Whatever the romantic images of the strong and self-sufficient heroes, of solitary and separated hermits, of isolates and rugged individualists, the truth is that somehow, somewhere, in the end, the human community takes everything to itself. "Alone we can do so little; together we can do so much," Helen Keller said.[42] We exist only in connection with the rest of the human race. We cannot stand alone. And yet, far too often we do.

We find ourselves alone in times of great stress, of great loss, of great personal pressure. We find ourselves in that spiritual space inside the self where no other can possibly come. Much as we would want them to do otherwise. Much as we try to communicate with the other, there is a wall of solid glass between us, apparently translucent but really opaque. Then we may look like we have touched another life but the touch, whatever its sincerity, is false. Every time we find ourselves saying "What I'm trying to say is...." or "No, what I mean is..." or "Why can't you understand what I'm saying...?" or "Are you listening to me...?" we are alone. Frightfully, irrevocably alone.

MEN OFTEN USE solitude to prove their manliness, to stake their bragging rights. Women never bluster about solitude. They can accept it in all the empty kitchens of the world. They can endure it through long, dark, frightening nights. But they seldom, if ever, choose it, they never glorify it and they always seek to fill it. Whatever can be done together can be borne. What must be done alone is impossible. For women, relationships—presence to the other—are of the essence of existence, the answer to isolation, the very marrow of their meaning.

There is in women's friendships a different quality of presence. Men, we have come to realize, conduct their friendships "side by side," in shared activities, in project development, in group play, in situations that bring no basic threat to power and demand no emotional vulnerability. Women, on the other hand, we now understand, shape their relationships "face-to-face," in mutual dependence, in honest conversation, in exposures of personal weaknesses.[43] Women carry within them to everyone they meet the power of the Veronica factor.

VERONICA IS A figment of the scriptures of the mind, a kind of Christian midrash on the Way of the Cross. There, centuries of oral tradition tell us, a woman by the name of Veronica looked on the bruised and bleeding body of Jesus as he struggled his cross up Golgotha alone. Then, in a burst of anguish for the pain she could not tolerate a second longer, she lunged out of the crowd, through the guard, and with a grandiose gesture of unmitigated compassion for the wounds of another, wiped away the blood on his face with a sweep of her own veil.

The Veronica story is midrash,

true, but that is not to say that it is nothing. Midrash, Judaism teaches us, is what the heart knows has gone on between the lines of scripture that scripture did not detail for the mind: Noah's fear, Abraham's confusion, Miriam's jubilation over the rescue of Moses, Joseph's anxiety, Mary's determination, Veronica's empathic presence. They all live clearly, certainly in the human heart, the truth for which no truth is needed. Veronica is the awareness in the Christian unconscious that "face-to-face" women face down pain. "Show me a friend who will weep with me," the Yugoslavian proverb teaches. "Those who will laugh with me I can find myself."

Veronica does not pretend to solve the problem but she refuses to ignore it.

The Veronica factor in friendship is itself a powerful one. Women look to other women to be the understanding, the empathy, the presence they need in matters of the heart too important to be overlooked in the process of living, too small to be noticed by the male world.[44] Veronica the friend takes off her own veil, exposes herself in society, to be a balm where there is only ache. Veronica does not pretend to solve the problem but she refuses to ignore it. She makes herself a clear and contradictory presence to the oppressive power structures around her, a confidante of impenetrable silence, a keeper of secrets, an anchor in the wind.

WOMEN WHO KNOW the call of Veronica in their relationships give great attention to the other without benefit of possessiveness or pettiness or expectations. Maude Preston writes of the experience: "There isn't much that I can do/ But I can sit an hour with you/ And I can share a joke with you/ And sometimes share reverses, too/ As on our way we go."[45]

In the Veronica factor of friend-ship, it is the staying power that counts, the awareness of awareness that carries a woman from one hard moment to another with an uplifting arm, an open mind. Women see a woman-friend as an equal, not as a partner who must be coaxed or coddled or persuaded or coerced before they can be made to listen, to understand.[46] A woman-friend is the one to whom a woman turns to understand the gravity of all the trivia of her life.

The Veronicas of our lives bring the power of affirmation to our pain. They confirm its reality, its injustice, and, in the end, its ultimate resolv-ability. With a Veronica at our side we can keep on walking, keep on carrying the weight of a day which only a moment before we found un-bearable.

It is important to realize, of course, that Veronica cannot extinguish the pain. She can only relieve it by the power of her presence. She brings the spiritual message: Don't give up; I am with you.

A woman-friend
is the one to whom a woman turns
to understand
the gravity
of all the trivia
of her life.

The Elizabeth Factor:

Acceptance

"IN MY FRIEND," Isabel Norton wrote, "I find a second self."[47] The comment brings us up straight. How many of those are there? Not many, surely. And what does that mean for the rest of the people in our lives whom we call "friend"? The statement becomes a rubric for telling one kind of relationship from another, for making an important distinction between a "friendly" and a "friendship" relationship. Best friends, very close friends, close friends, social acquaintances and casual acquaintances are not the same thing.[48]

Women, long-term research indicates, know the difference among them and treat all of them accordingly. Those who are, really, "a second self" are easily identified. Our friends, our "second selves," are the ones from whom we ask no explanations, on whom we pass no judgments. They are those whose struggles and stumblings, needs and responses we know like we know our own. Others we may spend time with, we may enjoy, we may join with in common projects but with them we do not expose our hearts in the hope of finding healing hands.

MOST OF ALL, our friends are the ones who take us into their lives with the ease of family and the warmth of love. They have no sarcastic comments to make of us, no subtle but clear criticisms to make in our presence for our sake, no noxious remarks to make to others about us. They offer what women say they look for most in a relationship: encouragement, support and a sense that they themselves are worthwhile human beings.[49] Real friends are simply there for us, no matter the pressure, no matter the pain. They are home for us when no other home is open.

It's not that friends justify our failures; it is simply that they do not even notice them. Failure has nothing to do with what they see in us. Failure has nothing to do with what we do or do not disclose to them. To a real friend, whatever sins we bear are simply the lessons we've learned along the way to becoming the best in us. There is no absolution needed. Where acceptance is the idiom of the heart, everything translates into understanding. A real friend, the second self, is cut from the cloth of Elizabeth.

ELIZABETH WAS the cousin to whom Mary of Nazareth went, betrothed, yes, but pregnant by someone other than Joseph "before they came together."[50] And unmarried. It was a major issue, both religious and social. To be pregnant and unmarried in the Jewish community of the time was not simply to risk disapproval, it was to risk death. It was certainly to be shunned. But Elizabeth, contrary to all tradition, against all common sense, took Mary into her home, no questions asked, no verdict levied.

More than that, Elizabeth recognized in Mary the great gain that would eventually come from a situation that

> Real friends are simply there for us, no matter the pressure, no matter the pain.

looked like such great loss to everyone else. Elizabeth accepted Mary for who she was and she saw the goodness in her. Literally.[51] Immediately.

THE ELIZABETH FACTOR in friendship is a fierce commitment to hold on with hope to the spiritual fecundity of a friend. However dark, however debilitating the circumstances with which the friend may be grappling at the moment, Elizabeth knows that in the end will come goodness because goodness is of the essence of the one we love as we love ourselves.

Acceptance is the ability to receive with a listening heart the friend who contravenes the social language of the time. The one who dresses differently, and talks differently, and lives differently from the norm of the neighborhood, the confines of the community. But the Elizabeths who love us take no notice of these differences. Acceptance of the differences in the other leaves room for the presence of the person and, as a result, she herself has room to become a new person.

WHAT WE ACCEPT into our lives in the other changes our own sense of what life is really about. For that reason, acceptance is never merely tolerance, it is vision. It is the new juice of soul that comes from understanding. It is what stretches my own spirit beyond the truisms of yesterday. Acceptance is its own reward. Anna Akhmatova says of it:

"If all who have begged help
From me in this world,
All the holy innocents,
Broken wives, and cripples,
The imprisoned, the suicidal—
If they had sent me one kopeck
I should have become 'richer
Than all Egypt'...
But they did not send me kopecks,
Instead they shared with me
their strength,
And so nothing in the world
Is stronger than I,
And I can bear anything, even this."[52]

IT IS THE ELIZABETH factor in friendship that separates the friendly from the friends, makes a chain nothing as meaningless as the unconventional or the unorthodox can break.

Acceptance is the universal currency of real friendship. It allows the other to be the other. It puts no barriers where life should be. It does not warp or shape or wrench a person to be anything other than what they are. It simply opens its arms to hold the weary and opens its heart to hear the broken and opens its mind to see the invisible. Then, in the shelter of acceptance, a person can be free to be even something more.

Acceptance is the universal currency of real friendship. It allows the other to be the other. It puts no barriers where life should be. It does not warp or shape or wrench a person to be anything other than what they are. It simply opens its arms to hold the weary and opens its heart to hear the broken and opens its mind to see the invisible.

The Anne Factor:

Nurturance

"FRIENDS SHOULD consider themselves," Anna Letitia Barbauld wrote, "as the sacred guardians of each other's virtue."[53] Friends give us something to live for when all the routine works of life have lost their savor or gone to dust. Friends give us something for which we are responsible until time takes them away or space removes them forever beyond the sound of my voice or outside the grasp of my hand.

It is not a passive exercise, this thing we call friendship. To have a friend is to have the duty to be one. If friendship is gone about properly, seen as a position of trust, lived in the hope of fullness of soul, and practiced as both pledge and possibility, it is an enterprise of personal development that runs the risk of changing both ourselves and our friend. It says, "I will nourish your dreams and prod all the potential that is in you." I will, in other words, nourish your life as my own. "Friends," Thoreau wrote, "do not live in harmony, but melody. We do not wish for friends to feed and clothe our bodies, neighbors are kind enough for that—but to do the like office to our spirits."[54] It is the quality of soul behind a friendship that tests its mettle and gives value to its weight. To nurture the other is to suckle their souls, to raise the sap of life in them, to bring them to ripe.

A GOOD RELATIONSHIP, the soul of a friendship, we are told, rests on six qualities. It gives a sense of security. We know that we are not alone in life. It provides a consciousness of social belonging. We know that given this friend we now have a welcome place in the groups of which we are a part. It holds a reassurance of personal significance. We know that we are worthwhile because there is someone who thinks so when we ourselves doubt it most. It implies a promise of assistance. We know that if something happens to us that someone, somewhere will wake to the sound of the phone, will come to help us when the room needs painting or the dead need grieved. It opens up the prospect of guidance. We know down deep that when we are confused there is someone who will help us thread our way through the maze. And it fulfills the need for nurturance.[55] We look for someone who will help us to become, to grow.

But to know what it means to be cared for, to be treasured, to be nurtured is to know the Anne factor in friendship.

ANNE, ACCORDING to tradition, was the wife of Joachim and the mother of Mary. She's an obscure figure. Anne is known only through the apocrypha, the unofficial gospels of the early church, but real in the mind of any woman who seeks to touch the spirit of the women who are her ancestors in the long, plodding endgame of life. Anne becomes the mother of that whole long line of women who look to Mary of Nazareth, the mother of Jesus, as a model of courage and endurance, of integrity and goodness. Anne is the root that nourished the tree. In looking to Mary as a model, we must look at Anne, as well. It is Anne who nurtured Mary to become who she was. It is the Annes in our own lives, that bevy of invisible women, who have nourished us, as well.

THE ANNE FACTOR in women's friendships is the emptying out of self that one woman does for another so that the steps of the friend may walk a smoother path than her own has been. It is the Anne factor at work when one woman teaches another how to bake bread and bathe babies and operate a computer and write proposals and apply for a position she feels sure she can never merit. It is the Anne factor that leads one woman to mentor another. And it is the Anne factor that reminds us of what it means to stand on the shoulders of the matriarchs who have gone before us, anonymous and invisible and uncomplaining. Because of what they gave to us unseen, we pour out ourselves on our friends. We live in the tradition of those women who prepared the way for us. Invisibly, often. Immeasurably, sometimes. Unreservedly, always. And one day, sooner or later, we ourselves all become Anne, the nurturer.

But nurturance is no small task and it must never be confused with control or superintendency or superiority. To nurture is not to dominate. It is to enable. It is to make the person I nurture free of me. "If we would build on a sure foundation in friendship," Charlotte Brontë wrote, "we must love friends for their sake rather than for our own."[56]

TO NURTURE A person is not to impose upon them a framework that, however healthy, is foreign to their soul. To nurture is to unleash the self for growth that is its own. Friendship nurtures when it provides a person the opportunity to experiment with the self and traces a watermark by which to measure the achievement. I become more of what I am by measuring myself against someone else. I do not become what I am by being directed by them. That is superintendency.

The one who nurtures me urges me on to aim for marks beyond me, holds nothing back, asks no return for the prodding but the effort of the try. The nurturer honors my self.

The Anne factor of friendship is

> To nurture is to unleash the self for growth that is its own.

to bring a person to see beyond their own limited sense of self to the sight that the other can see for them far beyond it. The nurturer indicates the path, points the way and then releases the friend to their own instincts. Anything else is control, not nurture. The nurturer begins a process for which she knows no end and which only the person herself can complete.

Most of all, the nurturer does not direct; the nurturer applauds what is already there to such a degree that the person I call my friend is carried along by the sound of my clapping to peak performance in the role that is her life. Then, if we have nurtured well, the friend becomes more than either of us ever expected. And that is the test of nurturance. "Anybody can sympathize with the sufferings of a friend," Oscar Wilde said, "but it requires a very fine nature to sympathize with a friend's success."[57] Those who nurture well, applaud the longest.

The Anne factor

in women's friendships

is the emptying out of self

that one woman does for another

so that the steps of the friend

may walk a smoother path

than her own has been.

The Mary Magdalene Factor:

Trust without Measure, Love without End

SOMEONE SOMEWHERE has written: "A friend is someone who knows the song in your heart and can sing it back to you when you have forgotten the words." Someone somewhere has clearly understood what real friendship is all about. My friend is the person who knows me as well as I know myself and holds that treasure, with all its soulfulness, all its struggle, in soft and tender hands.

Real friendship, then, requires two things: the transparent disclosure of the self and another's single-minded appetite to hear it and abiding commitment to treasure it. It means that I must be willing to be known and that someone somewhere must be intent on knowing me. Then, in those long, hard times when life is shale and rain, when I forget who I am and where I'm going, this other side of me brings me home to myself again. Friendship is not mere companionship. Friendship is intimacy.

Aristotle said that there are three kinds of friends: those we cultivate for the sake of the good times they give us, those we seek out for what they can do for us and those we love for their own sakes.[58] "If I were pressed to say why I love him," Montaigne wrote of his deceased friend Etienne de Boetie, "I feel my only reply could be 'Because it was he, because it was I.'"[59] Friendship, real friendship,

50

in other words, is the blurring of two souls into one where it was thought two had been. No price exacted. No interest paid.

FRIENDSHIP IS THE linking of spirits. It is a spiritual act, not a social one. It is the finding of the remainder of the self. It is knowing a person before you even meet them. I am not so sure, then, that we so much find a friend as it is that friendship, the deathless search of the soul for itself, finds us. Then the memory of Mary Magdalene becomes clear, becomes the bellwether of the real relationship.

MARY MAGDALENE IS the woman whom scripture calls by name in a time when women were seldom named in public documents at all. She is, in fact, named fourteen times—more than any other women in the New Testament except Mary of Nazareth, the mother of Jesus, herself. She is clearly a very important, and apparently a very wealthy woman. Most of all, she understood who Jesus was long before anyone else did and she supported him in his wild, free-ranging, revolutionary approach to life and state and synagogue. She was, it seems, the leader of a group of women who "supported Jesus out of their own resources."[60] And she never left his side for the rest of his life.

She was there at the beginning of his ministry. And she was there at the end. She was there when they were following him in cheering throngs. And she was there when they were taking his entire life, dashing it against the stones of synagogue and state, turning on him, jeering at him, shouting for his death, standing by while soldiers poked and prodded him to ignominy. She tended his grave and shouted his dying

Friendship
is
the
linking
of
spirits

glory and clung to his soul. She knew him and she did not flinch from the knowing.

The Magdalene factor in friendship is the ability to know everything there is to know about a person, to celebrate their fortunes, to weather their straits, to chance their enemies, to accompany them in their pain and to be faithful to the end, whatever its glory, whatever its grief. The Magdalene factor is intimacy, that unshakeable immersion in the life of the other to the peak of ecstasy, to the depths of hell.

INTIMACY IS a dangerous thing. It comes in two flavors: pleasure and truth. The intimacy of pleasure is self-serving and exploitative. It takes from the other the most private of gifts for the sake of the self. It is the taking of the secret for the pleasure of retelling it, it is the taking of affection for the sake of satisfaction, it is the taking of the gift for the sake of being embellished, it is the taking of the other for the stature of the self.

The Magdalene factor in friendship is what distinguishes those who walk with us through the shallows of life from those who take the soundings of our soul and follow us into the depths of them. For women, intimacy is a very serious thing. The mere act of sexual exploration will never substitute for it. Nor will the simple act of self-revelation. The first may be sheer release, superficial in its bonding, short-lived in its meaning. That kind of intimacy can exist in the most destructive of relationships. The second may be nothing more than exhibitionism, the spewing forth of the self with no real concern to be heard, only the desire to be on view.[61]

THE INTIMACY OF TRUTH, the Magdalene factor, is about appreciation, affection and warmth.[62] It is as important to the married as to the single, to the elderly woman as to the young.[63] It is about being deeply valued, reverently respected, lovingly tended and warmly received. It is about more than the present moment, more than the daily routine of partnership; it is about the obscure miracles and the hidden meanings of life. It is about forever. For these things, women often look to other women, to the Magdalenes of their lives, who stand by, who reach out, who watch, and who, whatever the delay, whatever the dearth of words, are content always, always to wait.[64]

"My fellow, my companion, held most dear," Mary Sidney Herbert wrote, "my soul, my other self, my inward friend."[65] It is, in its essence, intimacy. It is one common vision in two people so attuned, so in harmony, that whatever the uncertainty of the way, one thing is sure: This is a redeemable bond, a nexus of spirits fit for both the doubts and the iridescence of dark nights in deep woods.

The Magdalene factor
is intimacy,
that unshakeable immersion
in the life of the other
to the peak of ecstasy,
to the depths of hell.

The

Women

at the

Foot

of the

Cross

Epilogue

IT IS NOT EASY to find models of women's friendships. By and large they do not exist, lost like so much else of the history of women to the dust of time, underestimated in their own times, unnoticed throughout time, but never far from the surface, always the collagen of the woman's world. What we do have, however, is the data emerging in our own day to speak of their value, to describe their qualities. More than that, we have models of women who embodied the best in what women value in a friend. Lydia and her love for ideas, Prisca and her sense of self, Phoebe and her untiring support, Martha and her respect for experience, Veronica and her empathy, Elizabeth and her acceptance, Anne and her nurturance, Mary Magdalene and her undying intimacy. Out of these small shards of barely profiled lives emerge the pictures of every woman's love.

This small book is not meant to be anything more than the beginning of the cry to see the friendships between women as a strong power for good, a potential political force for the preservation of values that the world has greatly overlooked in favor of dominance and reason and individualism. But dominance has not saved us. And reason has been grossly unreasonable. Individualism made us cripplers of human community and has left us crippled ourselves, lost in a morass of solitary biases.

IT IS PRECISELY in their penchant for bonding, for tending, for befriending, for embracing, for the gathering of peoples that women's gift for the creation of human community becomes most clear. Women supported women at the foot of the cross then; women support women at the crossroads of life now. They care for one another's children, they cook one another's meals, they dry one another's tears, they applaud one another's gifts and they build up one another's spirits through one dashed dream, one hoping generation to the next. Mothers urge daughters to be more than they were ever enabled to be. Sisters hold up sisters when everything else in life conspires to hold them down. Women carry women friends down the rutted roads of a woman's life until the friend is strong enough to make the journey on her own. Women bind themselves to other women not as prisoners are bound but as mountain climbers are linked: on loose ropes designed to save but not control.

Life for a woman is far too commonly a long and lonely climb, often difficult, customarily overlooked. The contributions of women are seldom noted. The history of women and women's place in history is seldom told. The wisdom of women is, by and large, not anthologized, is, in other words, ignored. Despite the findings of modern psychology on the nature and quality of women's friendships, for instance, even the references in this book on friendship come most of all from men because it was men's works that were printed, published, taught across time. Those days are over. Women, and the rest of the world as well, are listening for the voices of women now.

LIKE THE WOMEN at the foot of the cross, the bonding of women through contemporary groups, organizations, social circles and public projects is now the breeding ground of a new kind of emotional life, personal development, re-creation and even the transformation of public institutions. Women's groups expand the definition of women beyond the domestic arena to full public participation and voice.[66]

Women's friendships and women's penchant for openness, possibility, support, empathy, personal experience, nurturance, acceptance, and intimacy are new hope for the human race. If we can only recognize them, if we can only bring them to life—respected, revered and invested with honor—in the world around us. For friendship is far more than a personal gift. The right friendship, rightly given, has the power to change the world. Or, as Albert Schweitzer said, "Sometimes our light goes out, but it is blown again into flame by an encounter with another human being. Each of us owes the deepest thanks to those who have rekindled the light."[67]

Endnotes

The Scripture references are from the New Revised Standard Version Bible: Catholic Edition © 1993 and 1989 by the Division of Christian Education of the National Council of the Churches of Christ in the U.S.A. Used by permission. All rights reserved.

[1] Ecclesiastes 4: 9-10.

[2] Cicero, *On Old Age and On Friendship*, Frank O. Copley, trans., (Ann Arbor: The University of Michigan Press, 1967), 49, III.

[3] Michel de Montaigne, *Essays*, Book One, Chapter 28, "On Friendship," J.M. Cohen, trans., (New York: Penguin Books, 1958), 95.

[4] Bryan Patrick Maguire, *Friendship and Community: The Monastic Experience, 350- 1250,* (Kalamazoo, Michigan: Cistercian Publications, Inc., 1988), 97.

[5] Ibid., xxxviii.

[6] Ibid., 92, 149.

[7] Ibid., 141-151.

[8] Diogenes Laertes, *Lives of Emminent Philosophers*, "Aristotle," bk. 5 sct. 20.

[9] *The Norton Book of Friendship*, Eudora Welty and Ronald A. Sharp, eds., (New York: W.W. Norton & Company, Inc.,1991), 87.

[10] Maguire, Introduction.

[11] Ibid., 45.

[12] Ibid., 50.

[13] Joan Chittister, *The Rule of Benedict, Insights for the Ages,* (New York: Crossroad, 1993), 67.

[14] Maguire, 300-335.

[15] Ibid., 380-407.

[16] Anais Nin. *The Friendship Page*. Hp. May 28, 2000. Online. Global Friendship. Available: http://www.friendship.com.au. May 28, 2000.

[17] Emily Dickinson. *The Friendship Page*. Hp. May 28, 2000.

[18] George Eliot. *The Friendship Page*. Hp. May 28, 2000.

[19] Patrick O'Connor, *Friendships Between Women: A Critical Review* (New York: Simon and Schuster International Group, Harvester Wheatsheaf, 1992), 2.

[20] Edith Deen, *All of the Women of the Bible,* (New York: Harper and Row Publishers, 1955), 221-226.

[21] Ibid., 224.

[22] Attributed to Confucius by Henry David Thoreau, "A Week on the Concord and Merrimak River," in Welty and Sharp, 513-519.

[23] Maguire, 67, 74.

[24] Contarello and Volpato (1991) in O'Connor, 7.

[25] Acts 1:18-24.

[26] Miguel de Cervantes in *Don Quixote de la Mancha.*

[27] Kahlil Gibran. *The Friendship Page*. Hp. May 28, 2000.

[28] See the work of La Gaipa (1977) and Fischer et al (1977) cited in O'Connor, 22-26.

[29] L. Tiger, *Men in Groups,* (New York: Random House, 1969), 2.

[30] O'Connor, 16-22.

[31] O'Connor, 13-16.

[32] Romans 16: 1-2.

[33] P.H. Wright, "Men's Friendships, Women's Friendships and the Alleged Inferiority of the Latter," *Sex Roles,* 8 no. 1 (1982), 1-20.

[34] Alexander Pope, "To Jonathan Swift," in Welty and Sharp, 106.

[35] Adrienne Rich, "Women and Honor: Some Notes on Lying," paper read at Hartwick College, New York, June 1975 (first published 1977; reprinted in

On Lies, Secrets, and Silence. New York: W. W. Norton, 1980), 191.

36 Plutarch in *On Friendship: A Selection*, Louise Bachelder, ed. (New York: Peter Pauper Press, 1966), 30.

37 Weiss (1969-74) in O'Connor, 5.

38 John 11:27.

39 Oliver Wendell Holmes in Bachelder, 5.

40 *The Great Quotations*, George Seldes, ed. (Secaucus, New Jersey: The Citadel, 1983), 64.

41 Richard Wilbur, "What is the Opposite of Two?" in Welty and Sharp, 196.

42 Helen Keller in *The Last Word: A Treasury of Women's Quotes*, Carolyn Warner, ed., (Englewood Cliffs, New Jersey: Prentice Hall, 1992), 133.

43 Wight (1982) in O'Connor, 29.

44 M. Komarovsky, *Blue Collar Marriage,* (New York: Vintage Books 1967).

45 Maude V. Preston in Warner, 137.

46 Gouldner and Syhmons Strong (1987:71) in O'Connor, 73.

47 Isabel Norton in Warner, 137.

48 Kurth (1970) in O'Connor, 23.

49 P.H. Wright, "Toward a Theory of Friendship Based on a Conception of the Self," *Human Communication Research*, 4 (1978), 196-207.

50 Matthew 1:18.

51 Luke 1: 41-45.

52 Anna Akhmatova, "If All Who Have Begged Help," in Welty and Sharp, 178.

53 Anna Letitia Barbauld in *The Quotable Woman: Eve to 1799*, Elaine Partow, ed., (Englewood Cliffs, New York: Facts on File Publications, 1985), 266.

54 Henry David Thoreau, "A Week on the Concord and Merrimack Rivers," in Welty and Sharp, 515.

[55] See R.S. Weiss (1969) "The Fund of Sociability," Transaction/Society, 6: 36-43 and R.S. Weiss, (1974) "The Provisions of Social Relationships," in *Support Systems and Mutual Help,* Z. Rubin, ed., (London: Grune and Stratton).

[56] Charlotte Brontë in Warner, 135.

[57] Oscar Wilde in Bachelder, 44.

[58] Aristotle, *The Nicomachean Ethics*, Chap. 4, sect. 5 (written c. 340 B.C.).

[59] Montaigne, 97.

[60] Luke 8:1-7.

[61] Gerard Egan, *You & Me: The Skills of Communicating and Relating to Others* (Belmont, California: Wadsworth Publishing Co. 1977), 51-60.

[62] V.S. Helgeson, P. Shaver and M. Dyer, "Prototypes of Intimacy and Distance in Same Sex and Opposite Sex Relationships," *Journal of Social and Personal Relationships*, 4 (1987) 195-233.

[63] O'Connor, 56-145.

[64] C. Goodenow, C. and E.L. Gaier (1990) "Best Friends: The Close Reciprocal Friendships of Married and Unmarried Women," unpublished paper quoted in O'Connor, 15.

[65] Mary Sidney Herbert in Partow, 125.

[66] O'Connor, p. 181-183.

[67] Albert Schweitzer, Quotez. Hp. August 2, 2000 Online. Available: http://business.virgin.net/mark.fryer/intro.html. August 2, 2000.

Appendix A

Artist's Explanation of Icon Symbols

About Icons

The word "icon" comes from the Greek word *eikon* meaning "image." It usually denotes religious paintings on wooded panels in the Byzantine style, either Greek or Russian.[1] Using age-old rules and traditions, icons do not depend upon the imagination and taste of the iconographer, but "are handed down from generation to generation in obedience to venerable traditions."[2]

When we speak of an iconographer's work it is correct to say "write" an icon, not "paint" an icon, clearly expressing the very idea that iconography is analogous to writing. Viewing an icon also contrasts to what is more familiar of the art of the West. They do not immediately speak to our senses. They are not intended, in other words, to force an emotional response.

Icons are said to be "holy doors."[3] They form a door into the divine realm, "a meeting point of divine grace and human need" where we may enter more deeply into our own interior life.[4]

Lydia

Lydia's right hand is depicted in a traditional blessing position. The position of her fingers is significant. They form the abbreviated name "Jesus Christ" (IX XC). The index finger is straight and the middle finger is slightly bent, forming the letters IC. The ring finger is bent down and the thumb passes across it to form the X, while the little finger is bent to form the C. This bless-ing position indicates her conversion and radical belief in Jesus Christ.

In Lydia's left hand is a chalice. As head of a house church (using the hermeneutics of reconstruction), it is appropriate to place in her hands a symbol of the bread and wine shared when the early church communities met. This Eucharistic symbol is recognizable today, and when placed boldly in the hands of a woman, it announces the rightful leadership positions women have always had in the creation of Christian communities, yet is denied them in the Church today.

Prisca

Prisca's right hand forms the blessing position, only this time her hand is facing inward. In her left hand are the words "Pursue Peace with Everyone" taken from the Letter to the Hebrews, 14:1. A text from Hebrews is significant because Prisca herself is one of the contenders for authorship of that letter.

Phoebe

Phoebe, commended by Paul in his letter to the Romans, was "a woman of authority, responsibility, and influence, and Paul's patron."[5] As a patron, she would have had some wealth and for that reason her veil is painted purple. She was said to have been a missionary and the one who delivered Paul's letter to the church in Rome, responsibilities not normally attributed to a woman. That is why the scroll she holds has a verse from the Letter to the Romans (Chapter 8) that is full of hope: "Nothing can separate us from the love of God in Christ Jesus."

Martha of Bethany

Martha's left hand is in the "showing" stance. Her right hand holds the Orthodox cross, commonly found in the hands of icons of saints. It is a bold position of a woman who proclaims Jesus as Messiah and means it.

Veronica

Veronica is painted as an older, wiser woman. She holds the veil she used to press upon Jesus' face as he carried his cross on Golgotha. In the Eastern Church, this image of Jesus is an often-painted one. It comes from the legend of King Abgar of the Syrian city of Edessa who sent a message to Jesus asking for healing. Jesus, the legend continues, pressed his face to the cloth, miraculously imprinting his image upon it, and sent it to Abgar. When the king received the cloth he was healed. Because this image of Christ miraculously appeared on the cloth, it is called the image "Not made by hands," or "Mandylion," the Greek word for cloth.[6] It is believed that this is the legend which the Western Church took and applied to a woman, to Veronica.

Elizabeth

Elizabeth is portrayed in her relationship to Mary, not in her role as the mother of John the Baptist. Here she stands alone, not in relation to her husband Zachary or her son John. The phrase written on her scroll announces her proclamation to Mary at the time of the "visitation" detailed for us in the Gospel of Luke.

Anne

Anne is the mother of Mary and the grandmother of Jesus. She holds a mandala of Mary, who in turn holds a mandala of Jesus to depict the maternal and matriarchal relationships of the women. Jim Forest says about the icon of Mary of the Signs (the prototype for this image) that it is "an icon of circles, symbols of wholeness and perfection."[7] Anne's robe is dark red which brightens in Mary's robe and again in Jesus' robe.

Mary Magdalene

In the Eastern tradition, it is told that after Jesus' Ascension, Mary Magdalene traveled to Rome. She was admitted to the court of Tiberius Caesar because of her high social standing. After describing how poorly Pilate administered justice at Jesus' trial, she told Caesar that Jesus had risen from the dead. To help explain the resurrection, she picked up an egg from the dinner table. Caesar responded that a human being could no more rise from the dead than the egg in her hand turn red. At that moment, the egg turned red.

Women at the Foot of the Cross

The women are *Salome* (mentioned in Mark, and referred to as "the mother of the sons of Zebedee" in Matthew), *Mary* ("the mother of James and Joses" in Mark, "the mother of James and Joseph" in Matthew, and " the wife of Clopas" in John), *His Mother* (in John), *Mary Magdalene* (mentioned in Mark, Matthew and John), and lastly, *His Mother's sister* (in John).

Salome and Mary (the mother of James and Joses and wife of Clopas) are both holding myrrh jars because along with Mary Magdalene they are mentioned as having gone to the tomb to anoint Jesus' body only to find the tomb empty, and in some accounts, to encounter the Risen Christ.

Mary Magdalene holds the Gospel Book and a scroll to symbolize her supposed authorship of the extra-canonical Gospel of Mary and her leadership role as preacher, evangelist and "Apostle to the Apostles."

"His Mother's Sister" stands with her left hand in the "showing" position. Lastly, Mary "His Mother" stands in the center of the icon in the "Mother of God of the Sign" position. This rendition proclaims not Jesus' birth (the traditional image), but his death with the cross in the mandala of her womb. It is an empty cross to symbolize that this community of women stands between Jesus' death and his resurrection and it is because of them that his rising from the dead was announced. Each figure holds a cross as a way of representing her presence at the crucifixion.

---

[1] Guillem Ramos-Poqui, *The Technique of Icon Painting*, (Harrisburg: Morehouse Publishing, 1990), 7.

[2] Henri J.M. Nouwen, *Behold the Beauty of the Lord: Praying with Icons*, (Notre Dame: Ave Maria Press, 1987), 14.

[3] Jim Forest, *Praying with Icons*, (Maryknoll: Orbis Books, 1997), 19.

[4] John Baggley, *Doors of Perception: Icons and their Spiritual Significance*, (Crestwood: St. Vladimir's Seminary Press, 1987), 4.

[5] Miriam Therese Winter, *Woman Word: A Feminist Lectionary and Psalter: Women of the New Testament*, (New York: Crossroad, 1995), 228.

[6] David Coomler, *The Icon Handbook: A Guide to Understanding Icons and the Liturgy, Symbols and Practices of the Russian Orthodox Church*, (Springfield: Templegate Publishers, 1995), 18.

[7] Jim Forest, 115.

APPENDIX B

Scripture References for the Women Cited in This Text

Lydia
Acts of the Apostles 16: 14-15

Prisca
Acts of the Apostles 18: 26
Letter to the Romans 16: 3-4

Phoebe
Letter to the Romans 16: 1-2

Martha of Bethany
Luke 10: 38-42
John 11: 17-44

Veronica
Luke 23: 27-29

Elizabeth
Luke 1: 5-25, 57-66, 39-45, 46-56

Anne
The Infancy Gospel of James/The Protovangelion
http://www.udayton.edu/mary/questions/faq/faq13.html

Mary Magdalene
Matthew 28: 1-10
Mark 16: 1-11
John 20: 11-18

Women at the Foot of the Cross
Matthew 27: 55-56
Mark 15: 40-41
Luke 23: 49
John 19: 25-26

—about the Author

JOAN D. CHITTISTER, OSB, is an internationally recognized lecturer, author and columnist with a background in education, social psychology, and communications. She has written 21 books including the recently released *Illuminated Life: Monastic Wisdom for Seekers of Light* and *The Story of Ruth: Twelve Moments in Every Woman's Life*. As lecturer, author, audio and video producer, and participant in numerous international seminars and delegations, Sister Joan brings to audiences around the world her reflections on women in church and society, human rights, peace and justice and contemporary religious life.

Sister Joan is the founder and executive director of Benetvision: A Resource and Research Center for Contemporary Spirituality.

—about the Artist

MARCIE BIRCHER, Benedictine oblate, "wrote" the icons in this book as part of her master's thesis/synthesis project at the Institute of Religion and Education and Pastoral Ministry at Boston College in 1999. A strong interest in feminist biblical studies drew her to these New Testament women and the artist in her soul led her to an "aha" moment when she realized that she could not "write herself out of the story" by producing a traditional written thesis. As a result, her experience of contemplative spirituality as well as her identity as a fine artist and a woman were brought together in this creative research project.

Marcie earned her bachelor of fine arts degree from Kent State University in 1980 and her master's in pastoral ministry from Boston College. Presently she is campus minister at two community colleges in Ohio.